GROWN

Little girl

Contents

Foreword 3

Jefferson Street—Sam 1988 5

Cottage Grove- Grease Fire 1990 9

South Bend Avenue- Christmas 1991 13

South Bend Avenue- Summer 1992 16

Johnson Street- Street Fight 1993 20

Johnson Street- I think I started….1995 25

Johnson Street- Over my Bed 1995 28

Homeless: Summer 1995 32

William Street- Girl, I ain't no Virgin no mo-1995 40

William Street- Fall 1997 8th Grade 50

William Street- Rat-Tail Comb – Late Fall 1997 52

William Street- Gone and Be with them People- Winter 1997 59

GROWN

Little girl

Collection of Vignettes, by Tarena Terry

Foreword

To the absent fathers of Janette's kids. I blame you for all the anger I projected on my mother, because although she had her faults you too should carry some of this guilt, but I'm sure you won't. You'll deny this guilt just like you denied your children. I always wondered what could have been if I had a father that was in my life, if my mother didn't have to struggle alone, if my mother hadn't turned to unthinkable habits to help her cope with the heartache, pain, and stress of raising three children on her own. She was just fifteen when she became a mother, and by the time she was twenty one she had three children, whom she tried to raise on her own. We went through some horrible shit that I wouldn't wish on my enemies. You swooped in during the holidays, the summers and occasional weekends and played savior, drop us off on Sunday and go back to your life of pretending you don't have responsibilities. I wasn't claim worthy in

1983 so let's keep it that way. Mama's Baby Daddy's Maybe never rang truer. To my mother, I love you, and I forgive you.

I'm the middle child of three, and this is my story.

Jefferson Street—Sam 1988

I remember living on Jefferson Street as a kid in a beautiful brick duplex. It was my mom, sister Twila, my brother Binky and me. We always had food, our apartment was nice, and we had decent furniture. Binky had his own room because he was a boy, so Twila and I shared a room. I loved showing off my dresses and skirts at school. My teacher Ms. Dawanna. always said "Tarena, you are the smartest little girl I know." Our life seemed normal. Most of the kids in the neighborhood lived with just their mom. On the weekends my mom's boyfriend, Sam, would come over. He always ordered pizza or brought us junk food. He and my mom drank and had a good time laughing and playing cards with their friends.

    One night; Twila was home watching me and Binky. She was eight, I was five, and my Binky was two. We were dancing in the living room to Michael Jackson's Billie Jean. Twila picked up a lighter and started playing with it. It looked pretty. She seemed like she knew what she was doing, so I kept dancing with Binky. She walked closer to the lamp shade. She got closer and closer, and it looked like the fire jumped from the lighter onto the shade, POOF! We stood there mesmerized, staring at the fire. The smoke alarms went off. We opened the doors in the front and back of our apartment and the windows.

Our mom must have been close because she came running in the apartment and put the fire out. She asked, "Who started the fire?" Binky and I pointed at Twila. Mom got an extension cord, yelling at Twila, "You were supposed to be watching them, and you down here trying to burn down our house and all our shit." As she whooped her, Sam came in and told my mom that was enough. She said, "Y'all need to get y'all ass to bed and stay there. I'll be down the street!" We were glad she was gone. I felt so bad for Twila. Her legs were red, and she had welts from the whoopin'. We cried ourselves to sleep that night.

We woke on Saturday morning, and Sam was still at our house; I liked when he stayed with us. He would tell me stories about how I was going to grow up and be a businesswoman and make a whole lotta' money. I wanted to be RICH! He said, "If you get your education, then you will be RICH! School will pay off, just stay in school." I was smart, I could read and do math, and I wasn't even in kindergarten yet. I knew I was going to be everything he said I would be. One day I would be a lawyer. The lawyer thing didn't work out, but his words stayed with me and served as motivation to grind for success.

Sunday came and went, and Sam was still at our house. It was nice having a man around; it felt like it was supposed to be this way all the time. On Monday, he told my mom he was going to take me to school. We went outside, I saw a motorcycle, and he said I was going to drive it to school. "Me? How cool! But I have on a skirt." He told me it would be all right, and he would make sure I was comfortable. He lifted me up and put me on the bike. I sat in front, he sat behind me, and my mom rode behind him. It was an awesome five-minute ride to my school around the corner, he even let me steer. He helped me off the bike and my mom checked me into school.

After school was over, my mom usually waited by the front of the school and we'd walk home. On that day, I wanted to get some penny candy from the barber shop with the dollar I got from Sam. My mom told me to get enough to share with Twila and Binky, I needed enough for us all, so I told them I wanted one hundred pieces. Although I was sharing, I had no intention of splitting this candy evenly, after all it was my money. Right before we got to our street, I saw a woman lying on the ground and foaming at the mouth. I asked my mom what was wrong with her. She said, "Oh she's just having a seizure, it will pass." I thought something else was wrong, but I was kind of scared, so we stepped over her and kept walking. Mom said we should mind our business, so I knew that the discussion and the concern was over.

When we got home, I gave my mom a permission slip for swimming. All the preschoolers were going to get swimming lessons and I needed $50 to participate. I knew that I probably wasn't going to get to go; my mom said she didn't have that kind of money, especially not for no damn swimming lessons. Head hanging, I went to my room and sat on my bed and cried. My mom came in and said she was going to page Sam and ask him for it. Whenever she paged him, she put in a special code so that he would know it was her. The phone rang, and I listened closely from my room because my mom was arguing with someone. "Look Josephine, I ain't got time to be arguing with you. Put Sam on the damn phone, he knows why I'm calling." Surprisingly, the tone changed. It sounded like she got through to him. "Hey, I need some money, these kids got field trips and I need to get some groceries, you gone come through and help me out? All right I'll see you tomorrow." She hung up; it sounded like I might be going swimming after all, but who was Josephine?

My mom always said that kids should stay out of grown folks' business, so I was always careful when I eavesdropped, didn't want to get caught or I'd get a whooping. Supposedly Josephine was Sam's wife, they had an entire family together, but her religion didn't tolerate divorces, so she dealt with Sam and all his shit through the years. She let it be known that she was his wife and made it a point to speak on the disrespect whenever it happened. But knowing my momma—she didn't give a damn about nobody's marriage. All she cared about was what she needed.

Cottage Grove- Grease Fire 1990

Just when I was starting to get used to our neighborhood and start to love my room, we had to move again. Mom didn't get along with the landlord on Jefferson Street, so they told us we had to find a new place to stay. It seemed like we never stayed anywhere longer than two grade periods. What I hated most about moving was that my mom always made us help her pack, carry things and unpack, we'd have to make new friends and find out where the parks and schools were in our new neighborhood. I always knew that a move was coming up if my mom started talking about wanting a fresh start, and she didn't want Sam or anybody else that wasn't worth shit to know where we lived. We moved into a small house on at the dead-end of Cottage Groves. I kind of liked it because we could play double-dutch and jump rope outside and not have to worry about getting hit by speeding cars. My cousins came over on the weekends and spent the night in the summer. We had so much fun playing hide-and-seek and barefoot racing in the street.

My mom's new friend Joe helped her find our new place. His in-laws owned the house, they lived on the street over from us, and he lived next door with his wife, Pam. He was nice and looked out for my mom because Sam was doing her wrong; one day Sam wanted to be with her, the next day he wasn't returning her pages to his beeper. By the time we moved we hadn't heard from Sam in months.

 One time Joe came out of my mom's bedroom zipping up his pants and adjusting his shirt. I followed him outside, and standing on the sidewalk in front of the entrance was his wife Pam. She wanted to know what he was doing in our house. He told her that he was helping to replace a light bulb that we couldn't reach, and the kids can't be up in there in the dark. I knew that was a lie. Don't no light bulb require you to take your clothes off. I knew they was in there acting a nasty. I heard them. Sooner or later we were going to have to move out of this house too. A few weeks later our landlords served us with an eviction notice. Urgh! I hated moving. We packed all our clothes and shoes in black plastic bags and put as much stuff as possible in boxes. I didn't even make it through the entire school year and I had just made friends. Now I was going to have to start all over again!

 A few nights before we moved out, my mom went out partying with my aunties. She told us not to open the door for nobody and to make a sandwich and eat some chips if we got hungry. We stayed up late watching Arsenio Hall, and then went to sleep. In the middle of the night we heard our smoke detector going off. When I opened our bedroom door, the house was full of smoke. I knocked on the closet door where Twila slept, and she jumped up and told me and

Binky to get on our knees and follow her to a safe space. We were so scared, and our mom was nowhere to be found. As we crawled through the thick smoke, we noticed that the light was on in our mom's bedroom, and it looked like it would be a safe place to stay because there was no smoke in there. We crawled in the closet, put blankets over our heads. Twila left me and Binky. She said she was going to go for help, and as soon as she opened the door my mom sprung up out the bed and staggered to the kitchen and said, "Oh shit it's a grease fire. I was frying some wings and must have lost track of time." She got a comforter and wrapped us in it and told us to stand in the backyard until she put out the fire; she said she it wasn't a big deal and could be taken care of with some salt.

When she went back in the house, Twila and I had asthma attacks, we didn't have our inhalers, they were in the house, but Mom went back in to get them. After we got our asthma under control our mom told us to climb in the car because that's where we'd be sleeping for the night. I felt guilty, we had gone over this multiple times at school—stop, drop and roll. We panicked and forgot everything we were taught and hid in a place that had no smoke but wasn't safe. We could have all died that night. Twila and I both knew our mom would never admit that the fire was her fault because she'd come home drunk and fell asleep while frying chicken.

South Bend Avenue- Christmas 1991

Sam had come back around, and I knew that married men were supposed to be with their wives, but it always felt good having him around. He always told us to go to college, and be somebody when you grow up. No one had ever spoke to us about anything beyond high school before. When Sam was around all of our bills were paid, and we had food, it made me feel good knowing I didn't have to worry about those things. When it was time to move again, Sam helped with our security deposit, our new house was on the Eastside on South Bend Avenue. I liked living there, because I *finally* had my own room. We had a living room *and* a dining room, a deck, and a *big* backyard. The yard was full of dirt, but it was *large*! Sam always seemed to come back when there was a crisis.

I turned eight a few days before Christmas, our house smelled good from baking peanut butter cookies with our mom and helping her prepare the cornbread dressing and greens. I remember going to bed and waking up early, knowing that we had a bunch of stuff that was dropped off from Christ Child, a program for families in need. They had an adopt-a-family program that my mom signed up for. I remember sitting with her at the kitchen table and making my list of what I wanted for Christmas, I asked for new clothes, shoes, a coat, and one toy—the only toy that I could think of wanting in the whole, wide world. A rollerblade baby doll, one that was a black girl and looked like me when my hair was straight. Once the gifts were dropped off on Christmas Eve, I just knew that one of those packages would contain at least one of the things I hoped for. Mom always came through for Christmas. I got to open my gifts first, because I couldn't contain my excitement. I got a new coat, panties and pajamas, new shoes and pants and the rollerblade baby doll. On top of it all, she was black. Oh, this is just what I wanted. I was crying. "Mom thank you so much I am so happy, I can't wait to see her rollerblade!" I turned to Mom, "Aren't you happy? What did you get?" She was in deep thought.

She blurted out, "Rob's daddy raped you when you were a baby. My cousin Rob's dad? I mean he molested you. I asked him to watch you while me and Anne went out clubbing. When the party was over, I came to pick you up and you were screaming at the top of your lungs. I had dropped your sister off with Mrs. Winston. Mrs. Winston was Twila's grandmother on her dad's side, we had different dads, she only watched *her* grandchild. Twila went to her grandmother's on scheduled weekends. I took you home, gave you a bottle and then went to change your diaper. When I opened it up, it was full of pee and there was lots of blood and you were swollen in your vaginal area. I took you to the emergency room, and they told me you had signs of sexual trauma! I just thought you should know."

I sat in silence, Indian style, shocked; my eyes filled with tears, and that's when I knew that Mom hated something about me. Why would she tell me this on Christmas, during one of the happiest moments of my life? I couldn't stand to be around her, I excused myself and went to the bathroom. I went to the full-length mirror across the room, took my panties off, and opened my legs, so that I could examine myself. Did I have any scars down there? Would I be a mom someday? It was then, in that moment, at eight years old, I became self-conscious about my body.

South Bend Avenue- Summer 1992

The summer of 1992 was a summer of freedom. I spent lots of time playing outside with the boys in the neighborhood, and a few girls who didn't mind getting dirty. I spent quite a bit of time in the South Bend Avenue projects, chasing my friends and playing tag. One day Brandon, a boy I liked, whispered in my ear that he wanted to play "Hide and Go Get It". I'd never played before, but I was all for new games. He told me to go hide and that he would come and find me. So, I hid in the best place I could. He counted to thirty and then my heart raced with anticipation that he would come and find me. I heard footsteps, but I was sure that I was hidden away pretty good, he tagged me, and I took off running. He looked upset.

He yelled, "You are not supposed to run when I tap you, we are supposed to kiss and hump."

"Huh? You want me to hump you?"

He said, "No, I want to hump you and kiss you."

So, I told him that I wanted to start over and that I would follow the rules. This time I intentionally hid somewhere I knew he would find me. I wanted him to kiss me and I wanted him to like me.

When he found and kissed me, I didn't know how to kiss, but I tried to kiss him back. I laid on the ground and he started grinding on me, but we had our clothes on. I liked it! It felt good, and I felt tingly all over. I wanted to play again, so we did.

Over the course of the summer a few other boys joined, and a couple other girls. There always seemed to be more boys than girls and it seemed that someone was always left with nobody to hump. I liked when they fought over who had dibs on finding me, it made me feel special. I liked a couple boys in the neighborhood, and they seemed to like me too! I just went with the flow, playing "Hide and Go Get It" throughout the summer with my friends. When I wasn't outside playing, I was at home doing my chores and eating so that I could go back outside and play.

Food always seemed to run low in the summer. Mom said that was because we were at home all day eating up every damn thing. We had fun at the park lunch meetups. Twila always thought she was too good to go to park lunches, but sometimes she asked me and Binky to bring her something back if they had something good. Me and Binky would go to park lunches every day except the weekend; the Parks and Recreation people don't serve food on the weekend, and if it rained, they didn't come either. I remember that they said after 4th of July they wouldn't be coming back to the park by our house for the rest of the summer so we would need to find another way to eat if we didn't have food at home.

My mom was getting ready to celebrate her twenty-seventh birthday and she told us that she was going to Chicago with our god mom for a couple days, but she would be back soon. It wasn't a big deal for her to not come home sometimes. We were used to it. Plus, Twila was going into sixth grade and we knew the rules—be in the house before the street lights came on, don't open the door for nobody and lock the doors. My mom left for her trip on her birthday, July 15th, and we went on like normal. The park lunches stopped a little over a week before, and we only had a little bit of bologna and chips, but it went quick. After a few days we thought Mom would be back, but she didn't come. People stopped by looking for her, but she wasn't there. We just told them that she was at the store or would be back soon, but she didn't come. We ate all the food and we were just down to some canned goods, pork and beans, green beans and beets, Yuck! I didn't want to eat that. We tried but it was so nasty. Binky said, "Should we just call Sam, maybe he can help us?" We didn't have his phone number, but we knew how to page him on his beeper, so we paged him and put in our mom's code—999. He called us back and ask for Mom. We told him she wasn't home, and he asked why we paged him. We told him she had been gone for over a week, and we were hungry and there wasn't any food in the house. He said, "I can't believe she went out of town and left y'all by yourselves, and she didn't leave no money or food? What the fuck is wrong with her? I ain't talked to your mom in weeks, but I will be by in an hour to take y'all to Martins to get some groceries." We were so excited we told him to just meet to us at Martins, we were going to travel on foot.

Me, Twila and Binky walked the thirty minutes to Martin's Supermarket. We were so happy Sam was going to get us some food! When we got there, he told us to get whatever we wanted with $50! We picked up lunch meat, microwaveable food, chips, hot dogs, bread, cereal, milk, and some Sunny Delight! He waited for us outside, we took our bags out to his car, and he drove us home so we wouldn't have to walk with all the bags.

A few days later Mom came home. It had now been two weeks. She looked tired, went to her room, and went to sleep. No explanation. She didn't even give a shit that we were home alone for weeks without an adult. We were her kids, should we not expect anything from her? Did she not realize that she is our *mother*? This bitch was out of her mind! She would often tell us that we were smart kids, she knew she wasn't always at her best, but if push came to shove we knew what to do in an emergency, but I was only eight years old I wasn't ready to deal with being neglected and hungry for two weeks, survival skills or not!

Johnson Street- Street Fight 1993

We left the Eastside because Mom said that our landlord didn't want to fix nothing but wanted to get paid. The basement was flooding, and we had some issues with our furnace and the roof, and she said she wasn't paying him a dime until he fixed everything that was broke. Well he told us that we had to go, so we packed up and moved to the Northside. I had to leave my best friend Tara, and Perley Elementary, and start all over again, way across town at a different school on the Northside, Eggleston.

    I didn't want to go to this school, and I didn't like the kids on my bus, but I met twins, Tiffany and Tasha, and they quickly became my friends. I never had twin friends before, and I was able to tell them apart. Twila was at a different school— Dickinson. She always made friends quickly but that also came with enemies, because of the boys that liked her. I recall this big girl named Shonda who lived a block away. She didn't like Twila, she was always starting shit. Matter of fact, everybody on her block was always starting shit. I didn't like nobody on Obrien Street. They hung outside and made fun of people and ran up on you if you said anything smart back to them. I hated walking past that street. Twila was out visiting her friends one day, riding down the street on her bike and Shonda's older sister pushed her to the ground.

Twila came home crying. My mom was so mad that she got out her bed, threw on some clothes, and told Twila to show her who put they hands on her. We walked to Obrien, and she pointed out the house that Shonda and her sister stayed in. Mom knocked on the door and told them to come out, because ain't nobody got no business putting they hands on her child. I don't know what was said next because I was on the sidewalk, but I knew it wasn't good because I saw fists flying, clothes coming off, and hair being pulled. My mom and sister disappeared into their house for a minute, and then I saw my mom dragging this tall girl out. She was bigger than her. By this time, my mom's boobs were out, but she didn't care, she kept on fighting. Then we heard police sirens. We ran back to our house a block away on Johnson Street. They pressed charges against my mom, saying that she was fighting a minor, she was seventeen; now this was another thing that was on my mom's record that she didn't need. There wasn't that big of an age gap, my mom was in her mid-twenties.

    A few weeks went by, and things seemed to go back to normal. I played with the twins, Tiffany and Tasha over on Huey Street, and Binky was playing with their brother Martez. Our mom called their dad and told us to come home because we had been at their house all weekend. We didn't want to go home but we had school on Monday so we couldn't stay any longer. Binky and I were walking down the street, we had to pass Obrien. I hated this street because I knew we would end up walking past Jasmine and Jessica. Jessica was in my class at Eggleston Elementary and Jasmine was her sister who was just a grade above us. They were popular at school but were also mean girls/bullies, and I thought they were my friends. One week they were my friends, the next week they wanted to fight me. I don't like wishy washy people; they were so fake I started to hate them. I told Binky we were going to walk past their street and not make eye contact. Well I guess they didn't like us that day. Jasmine took my bike and started wheeling it toward their house. We were outnumbered, so we ran home and told Mom, and she and her friend Mag were ready to go get my bike back. Twila and her friend Lisa came too. When we got to Obrien Street there were many people outside: Jasmine, Jessica, their mom and stepdad, and some guys we didn't know. My mom wanted to talk to their mom who obviously had no intention of talking. Their mom started talking crazy, so my mom punched her in the face. Their mom was an obese woman and taller than my mom. She picked my mom up and slammed her on the ground and got on top of her. Then Jasmine came after me, Twila stepped in to protect me and started fighting her. Jessica jumped in, and Lisa jumped in to help Twila. I was so scared. There was so much going on around me, I didn't know what to do, and I wanted to make sure my little brother didn't get hurt, but he was trying to fight too. He kicked their momma in the butt while she was on top of our mom and tugged on her shirt. I wanted to help but I was scared; everything happened so fast. Mom yelled, "Come on, let's go" and we all went back to our house. My mom was mad. Maybe she was mad at me because I didn't jump in the fight. I felt like I failed my family; even Binky had enough guts to jump in. My mom told us to get in the house and stay in there, so we did. She said she was going outside to make sure nobody was trying to come to our house to retaliate. She walked to the alley and I started walking outside, and I heard my mom yell, "Mag stay in the house with my kids, don't let them come outside." Three men ran toward my mom and she started swinging. They knocked her to the ground, and she balled up like a rolli polli. They were kicking and punching her, and I could hear her screaming for help, and that someone needed to call the police. We called the police. By the time they got to our house, which seemed like forever my mom was back in the house and really beat up. Her eyes were swelling up, and she had lots of sore spots. At that moment I knew that my mom lost something back there—her dignity and pride. She took those punches and kicks so that they wouldn't come in our house, and that's when Jasmine and Jessica were officially the top of my enemy list. That day will stay with me for many reasons. I'd never felt so betrayed by people I thought were my friends. But all of that was outweighed by what I felt for my mom. I was so happy because in her own way she acted like a mother. A good mother. My mother. She fought for her kids and proved to me that in her own way, she did love me.

Johnson Street- I think I started....1995

It was February, our mom had got a job at a nursing home and she was at work, so it was just me and Twila at home. Binky was somewhere playing with his friends. My stomach had been hurting all day, so I went to the bathroom to pee and all this brownish-red stuff was in my panties. I wiped myself until it was all gone and then told Twila. She came in to look and said, "Oh, I think you started your period." I was confused because I didn't know what to do; my mom never talked to me about when or how this would happen. We never really talked much about our bodies, but I knew about other girls my age getting their period. We called my mom at work and she got mad at us because it wasn't her break yet, and she said to just use some toilet tissue because she didn't get paid until Friday and I'd have to figure it out. I asked her if she had some pads and she said she was out. Then she said, "Why don't you call your friend Amber? I'm sure she has some she can let you borrow and then when Mom gets paid, we will give her some of ours." Amber met me at the corner and passed me three pads so that I could make it through the day; she said she didn't have a lot. I was happy that I had the few that she gave me. I felt confident that I would be able to get through the night and school tomorrow with the few that I had.

Later that night when my mom came home, I thought she was going to give me a hug, and we would talk about a girl's body and the changes we go through. But she told me that I needed to shower daily and change my pad often, and that I had to wait a few days until she got paid to get some Kotex. That was it. I thought it was going to be like the movie "My Girl" when Shelley talked to Vada about her period. She seemed like she cared and was nurturing with Vada. My mom did none of that, I wish she would have.

The next day, I got off the bus at Amber's house and told her thanks again for helping me, and then I was distracted by these bitches coming down the street. I knew something wasn't right—it was Jasmine and Jessica. Amber told me to hurry up and go home, but something just seemed off with how she was acting. Jasmine and Jessica got in my face and said they should beat my ass for telling everybody that they were trouble makers. I said, "You not gone touch me, you put your hands on me, I'm going to get my mom and Twila."

They said, "Go tell your mom with her poor crack-head ass, she can't even buy you no pads for your pussy!" I froze. I didn't know what to say. I was crushed. I looked at Amber, and then she chimed in and started teasing me with them. I thought she was my friend. How could she betray me, how could she tell them my business?

I stormed off. I'd never trust anyone else again. I didn't want to be her friend anymore, because if she wanted to team up with these tramps then she was never my real friend anyway. I was, embarrassed, and feeling lower than I'd ever felt before.

Johnson Street- Over my Bed 1995

I just got back from Mt. Vernon, Illinois from spending time with my dad, David, and his wife and her kids. Although the summer was dysfunctional as hell, it was better than what I'd be doing if I stayed home in South Bend. My dad was verbally and physically abusive to his wife, she always seemed to have a sore arm or bruises on her body. I remember hearing him body slam her because she said or did something he didn't like. I'm sure she was unhappy about the fact that he'd disappear on payday and come home hungover or high with no money. I thought he had it all together, after all he was married, lived in a nice house and seemed to have the family dynamic that I really wanted. Turns out, he was just as bad as my mom, except he had a wife to help him, meanwhile my mom had no one.

    At my dad's I didn't go hungry and I always had clean clothes, underwear, and my hair stayed braided. After a while, I was ready to go home and see Binky, Twila, and my friends. When I got back to South Bend, my aunt volunteered to drop me off. No one was home, but I got in the door and waved her off and reassured her I'd be okay.

    Our house looked deserted, there was rotten food in the refrigerator, maggots crawling around, and the electricity was off. The water was still running, and the phone was on. I went up to my room to find it completely messed up, and someone had smashed my piggy bank! I was so mad because I was looking forward to seeing how much money I had so I could buy something for back to school. I was disgusted to come back to this house. I sat on my bed and prayed that my dad would come rescue me and take me back with him. Then I heard my mom calling me from downstairs. "Rena! Are you up there?" I was happy to hear her voice, but concerned that she was so happy when everything was so messed up. After a big hug, she told me sister and brother were staying with friends, and that I could go stay with friends if I wanted to, or I could stay home. It was up to me.

I had just gotten out of the car from an eight-hour ride. I wanted to stay in my room and unpack. I didn't want to go to someone else's house. I went up to my room and lay down to take a nap. I left my mom and her friends downstairs; it looked like they were getting ready to start drinking. The central air was off, but I didn't care. I dozed off anyway. I was dreaming of being back in Illinois with my dad and stepmom. They had electricity, and they had food. I felt this warmness come over my body; I woke up! "What are you doing!? Who are you? Why are you in my room? Mom, Mom, Mom!" The company my mom just introduced me to a little while ago was standing over my bed. He had on corduroys, pants unzipped, penis out! He said he got lost and couldn't find the bathroom. "You Liar! The bathroom is before you get to my room." He told me to shush and that he wasn't going to take long and started pulling down his pants. I jumped up and pushed past him. There were seventeen stairs, I always counted, but I must have skipped some. I took four steps and was downstairs.

"Mom! This man was trying to rape me, he was in my room!" She called him Ellis. He came downstairs and said he was just trying to find the bathroom, and that it was all a misunderstanding. I could tell that my mom was high, she was too calm.

She said, "Ellis, please apologize to my daughter for scaring her." He apologized and she told me to go back to my room.

I was fuming. "You not gone put him out? You gone let him stay in our house after what he did?"

She said, "Well he said sorry, what else you want me to do?"

"I want him gone!" She didn't make him leave. I went upstairs and packed and went to stay at the twins' house for a few days. Before I returned home, I called my Granny Jewel, she was just *my* granny, my dad's mom. I told her what happened and she said sure as hell was going to tell my dad what was going on and if I didn't feel safe after I had some time with the twins that I could come stay with her until we got everything figured out.

I told the twins what happened to me, and they told me I should tell their dad Jay, he said my mom should be ashamed of herself having someone in her house that could harm her daughter. He looked at me and said, "You are always welcome over here, nobody gonna mess with you as long as I'm here." Jay was a single father. Tiffany and Tasha had their own issues with their mom to deal with but I've never seen a man so responsible and caring for his children and I knew that he meant what he said from the heart. I knew one thing, Twila and Binky were gone at the same time, I better find somewhere to go or else this could happen again.

It really hurt that my safety wasn't a priority for my Mom but anyone outside of the situation could clearly express concern for my well-being, all she cared about was what she wanted. I guess I have to look out for myself going forward, she always told us not to depend on anyone, I guess that meant her too.

Homeless: Summer 1995

Nothing was the same after my mom's mom died. We didn't get together with all of my aunts and cousins to have family dinners, or cookouts. Everyone kind of went their own direction, my aunts were struggling like my mom and were fighting to keep their families together, Most of my first cousins were either in foster care, juvenile detention or on the verge of being a runaway. My grandma was the glue that kept the family together, now we were acting like many, separate families instead of holding on to each other.

 We were staying at my godmom, Kim's house over the summer. We got kicked out of our house because our utilities kept getting shut off and Mom wasn't paying the rent, so now we were living on Calvert on the Southside. I loved being at my Kim's. She had food, cable, her utilities were on, and she was always nice to us, but I could never get comfortable there. I felt like there was some tension between her and my mom, but she never fussed about us staying with her. My mom was rarely there. She came to check on us and that was about it. One day my mom and Kim got into a fight and my mom said she was taking us with her. Twila stayed with Kim, but Binky and I went with our mom, we always preferred to be with her.

 My mom had my grandma Bobbie Jean's old navy blue station wagon. She took us to Rally's for burgers and fries and drove around just enjoying the summer day. We went to my cousins Doris and Tommy's house and hung out over there for a couple days. Eventually they started drinking and fighting and we had to leave. Since me and Binky knew our way around town, we asked Mom if we could go see our friends. I went to Tiffany and Tasha's house, they were in Chicago for a few weeks, but Martez was there, so I asked Jay, the twins' dad, if we could stay and play. As I was walking back to where my mom was, I saw Jasmine and Jessica, and they said they were sorry for being mean to me and that I could come over their house to play with them, and that I could spend the night if I wanted to.

They seemed sorry, and even though my mom and sister would be mad at me for going, I knew that their mom worked, they had food, and I had a place to lay my head. I know it's stupid to stay with the enemy, but I was desperate. I called my mom and told her where I was at and she didn't seem to mind. She said that there was no reason that us kids couldn't make up and be friends, even though the same wouldn't happen for her and their mother. Twila felt like she wanted a change of scenery as well and went to stay with her best friend, Myra. The three of us were in three different places. I think we were gone for like two weeks hanging out with our friends. I saw Twila and Binky a few times as we were all in the same neighborhood, just at different houses. Jasmine and Jessica knew all the boys in the neighborhood, so we hung out with them.

One night we were getting rides on mopeds and everyone was meeting up at Brad's house, Brad was a sophomore in high school, and one of the popular kids in the hood that dressed the best and threw the best parties. When we got over there everybody had somebody to hook up with except me. Then this dude named Bruce wanted me to hook up with him and I wanted to, but I was on my period and was using tissue as a pad to catch the blood, and I didn't feel comfortable kissing and making out with him. I told him I had to go outside and that I'd be back, but I never came back. I walked to Jasmine and Jessica's and their mom let me in. I told her that I left the party early and just wanted to lie down. She was nice to me. We talked about her childhood and she asked me where my mom, brother and sister were. She asked me why we weren't all together and I told her. She started crying.

She said, "If you need anything baby you can stay here if you want to, you are always welcome." I felt like everyone forgot about that fight, but I felt guilty for being there. I needed a place to stay, but it was hard to forget the attack on my mom in the back of our house.

The phone rang. It was my Twila. She told me to go get Binky from the twins' and to meet her at Myra's, because Mom was coming to pick us all up. I didn't have anything to pack up, because I had been

I was on honor roll twice during the time I was with her; she even showed up to my parent teacher conference, which my mom never went to. She came home from the conference and gave me a few dollars. She said I earned it, she couldn't believe all the awesome things my teacher had to say about my behavior and my grades; not because I wasn't capable, but because she couldn't understand how a child who had been through so much, could excel at school like that. She made me feel good about myself. I felt like I could do anything! Time went on, and it seemed like I would be staying with my granny long-term. I didn't have everything I wanted at my Granny Jewel's place, but I didn't have to worry about clean clothes, food, heat or lights and she had cable. I was perfectly content staying with her as long as she would have me.

About six months later, my mom showed up and said I had to come back with her, that she found a house and she wanted her kids back. She had this sense of entitlement that she could show up whenever she wanted, and make demands and everyone had to fall in line. I asked her, "Why now? Why do we have to come back with you? I'm doing fine here, and I'll be one less kid you have to worry about, it will be easier for you."

She said, "I'm not asking you, I'm telling you. I have a house and all my kids are going to be there with me. I'll be back in three days.

Lakeside. I gave him directions to Anne's and told him to call me when he got there. "Ask Anne if can you stay with her until Mom comes to find you, and I'm going to ask my granny if I can stay with her."

Binky said he didn't want to go, he wanted to stay with me, but I told him nobody was going to take two kids. Since he wasn't related to my dad's side of the family, I wasn't sure if we could stay together. He was sad and so was I, we didn't want to split up, but we needed help, we both needed to eat, and get cleaned up, and our options were better than staying in the car waiting on Mom. He was only eight, but I could tell that his brain was on overload and he understood what we needed to do. We hugged one last time and went opposite directions.

Granny Jewell wanted to know how I got to her house by myself, and where was Mom. When I was with her, I dreaded going home. Over the years my mom was very clear that we never talked about what went on in our house, and if we did, she would beat our ass. But I let it all out—all the pain, the hurt, and what happened today. She said I didn't need to say anymore, and I could stay with her until my mom got herself together. I ate a sandwich and some chips and lay down to go to sleep. When I woke, I called Anne to make sure that Binky made it safely to her house. I stayed with my granny for a few months. She didn't have a lot of space, but I had everything I needed.

food to help, she just disappeared like before. Kim grew impatient and went looking for Mom, and when she found her, they got into another fight and she told Mom she wasn't coming back to her house, and Mom said she was coming to get her kids. Me and Binky were ready to go with her, but Twila begged to stay with Kim, so Mom let her.

Mom took us to Linden Street on the West side, she went into this big vacant house and told us to sit in the car until she got back. It was hot in the car. We had all the windows down, but I felt like we were sitting there for a very long time. Binky was hungry and started crying, so I blew the horn. Mom came to the porch and told us to keep our damn hands off the horn and not rush her, she'd be out in a minute. I knew this place! There were dudes going in and out of the house that were the same age as Twila; this was a crack house! She got the nerve to be in there getting high while me and Binky sat outside in the heat, in the middle of summer, in this hot ass car! I was mad! I went to the porch and peeked in and saw my mom sitting on the floor. "We ready to go!" I yelled.

She said, "Leave then, I don't give a damn." I couldn't believe her! Why would she do us like this? Tears ran down my face, I walked back to the car and got Binky and told him that we had to split up if we wanted somebody to take us in. My granny Jewel lived a few blocks away on Florence, and our cousin Anne lived a few blocks away on the washing the same underwear over and over in the bathroom, and Jasmine and Jessica let me wear their clothes.

Mom came to Myra's to pick us up and she said that my grandma, her mother, Bobbie Jean had died. We all cried. We went to grandma's house on Napoleon street on the Eastside. The next morning, the landlord was knocking on the door, telling us that we had until the end of the day to get out. "My grandma just died, and you couldn't wait to put us out. We haven't even buried her yet!"

He said, "I'm sorry, this is a government house and if the primary tenant passes away then no one else can assume responsibility for this property." So, my mom started pulling out trash bags, said there was nothing we could do, and that we needed to put everything in bags that we could carry. A lot of our stuff was at Grandma's since we didn't have a place to stay. My mom still had the keys to the car, so we loaded up the station wagon and put all our things in the back and drove away. Twila went back to Kim's, and Binky and I stayed with Mom and we went back to Doris's until it was time for Grandma's funeral. Her funeral was on July 15th, the same day as Mom's birthday. Mom and Kim made up and afterwards we went back to Kim's for a few days, but the same problems between her and Kim arose again. She thought that losing my grandmother and being homeless would put things into perspective for my mom. My mom hadn't checked on us, bought any

You need to have your things packed and ready to go, and if you don't want to leave, I will make you!"

My granny said, "Regardless of what your mother has done, she is still your mother. You need to go be with her, you can still come see me on the weekends if you want to." I was sad, I didn't understand why my granny didn't fight to keep me, I really wanted to stay with her, but she always had a way of empathizing with people when they wanted another chance to get it right, and I felt like she was doing that with my mom. Their minds were made up and I had no choice but to prepare to move back with my mom and leave the comfort and security of my granny.

William Street- Girl, I ain't no Virgin no mo- 1995

In the fall of 1995, we lived on the Westside on William Street and we were in the Clay School District. Twila went to LaSalle because she wanted to be with her friends, Binky was still in elementary and attended Muessel, and I had just entered seventh grade and was officially a middle-schooler. This was the first time that all three of us were at three different schools. I wasn't somebody's little sister or somebody's big sister. I was just Tarena.

Me and my best friend Crystal hung out regularly after school. We talked about the boys we liked and about girls that didn't like us, and the struggles we had with our moms, her mom was in prison, and of course my mom had her addictions to drugs and alcohol. She lived with her granny permanently. We shared our secrets with each other. One day in English class, Crystal told me that she had lost her virginity over the summer to her crush, Sean. I gasped. I felt betrayed. We had vowed that we both would wait until marriage because we didn't want to get pregnant like our moms and be teenage mothers with kids we couldn't take care of.

I was really concerned for her and asked what made her decide to "do it". Did it hurt? Did it feel good? Where did y'all do it at? Is he your boyfriend now? Was there a lot of blood? Did he use a condom? What if you get pregnant? She was like, he kept asking me to do it, so we did it in the garage so my granny wouldn't catch us. Yeah it hurt, it's supposed to hurt the first time, but after a while it started to feel good. There was a little bit of blood, like spotting but it wasn't that bad. "For Real? Wow, so this happened right before school?" She was like no, we've been "doing it" for about a month. Again, I felt betrayed, how could my best friend do something like this, without telling me first? We were supposed to wait until we got married, or at least both "do it" around the same time, so we could be non-virgins together! Well, if she already did it, maybe I should too? I didn't want to be left out. Listening to the other girls from in the cafeteria and in the hallways, a lot of them were already doing it. I guess I was holding out for a little while longer, but the boys only wanted the girls that were giving it up, and no one liked me. A month went by, Crystal was spending more time with Sean, so I made new friends.

    I started hanging out with a girl named Joanna. I heard she knew a lot of fine dudes and she could hook me up with somebody cute. Joanna was two years older than me and apparently got held back. She was already having sex and it was a rumor that she had several miscarriages. We talked a little about school and a lot about boys during our late-night chats on the phone. One day she called me on three-way with this dude that she said was like a big brother to her. His name was Greg Prince and he sounded like he was fine, with a deep voice that made him sound mature. I gave him my number at the end of our call, and he started calling me without Joanna. Only problem is, he lived on the Northside and I lived on the Westside.

One day he was like, "My granny goes to the church by your house. She has to go to a meeting and I'm going with her, let's meet me up there." I met him and we walked around, held hands and then he told me he wanted to go to the park behind the church. We went to the park and swung on the swings, and then he said we should climb in this jungle gym. We were making out and rubbing on each other, he asked me if he could finger me, and even though I didn't know what that was, I didn't want to appear lame, so I said okay. He fingered me, and his hands were kind of dry and it hurt. He said I must not be turned on or ready to go to the next level. I mean I liked him, but was that the next level? We hadn't even been dating that long, if this was dating? He suggested that we skip school the upcoming Wednesday because at his house we would have privacy and a comfortable room to "do it" if I wasn't scared. Scared? Who me? Nah, I ain't scared. I told him I'd let him know if I could make it.

Wednesday was perfect. My mom had a new job and had to be at work early and wouldn't see me leave the bus stop before the bus came. I kept walking and jumped on the Transpo to take me to the Northside. I got off on Elwood across from the Mini Mart. My heart was beating so fast. He said he lived in the yellow government house, he told me to go to the back door so his nosy neighbors wouldn't see me go in the house.

When I finally got inside, he wasted no time putting the moves on me. We started kissing. I put my books down on the table and we went upstairs. His cousin, Desmond, was in his room playing video games.. I sat on the bed across from his cousin, Greg pulled me closer. I told him I didn't feel comfortable making out in front of his cousin. So we went under the covers. I asked him to pull the covers all the way over our heads because I didn't want to see his cousin. So, he pulled down my pants and my panties and tried to stick it in, and it wouldn't go in. Then he licked his fingers and tried again. He was slow, and then he kept adding pressure firmly, I was holding my breath, and my eyes were closed tight, I tensed up, he told me to relax, it finally went in. Thank goodness, whew that hurt! But I was glad the hard part was over. The entire time he was humping me I was wondering when it would start to feel good because it didn't feel good, it just hurt. When he was done, I got up, pulled up my clothes and went to the restroom. I wanted to see how much blood there was. I was worried there would be blood on the bed and that him and his cousin would make fun of me, luckily there wasn't any on the bed. I peed and wiped and there was just spotting. I hung out for a little longer, his cousin was making me uncomfortable the way he was staring at me, I decided that it was time to go, since school was going to be out soon, and I needed time to get my plan together so I didn't get caught.

I skipped school again a few weeks later. We had the same routine as before. I entered through the back door, dropped my books on the dining room table, and went to his room. As soon as I opened the door, another part of the routine, his damn cousin was there. As usual, he watched us and pretended that he was playing video games. When we were finished Greg asked me if I liked his cousin.

"Hell naw, I'm not fucking him! Why would you ask me something like that?" I responded.

"Well, he likes you, you should let him get some."

"Some of what?"

"You, know, let him hit it."

My heart sank. This was my boyfriend, the dude I lost my virginity to. How could he ask me some shit like that? I was offended. I started cussing and crying. Just like that, I felt like I meant nothing. Desmond was like, I'll be gentle, we know you not a ho, I just want to see what it feels like to be with you. Gentle my ass! He started walking toward me. I was scared. Then all the sudden from downstairs we heard, "Greg! What are you doing home from school? You bet not have nobody in my house."

Oh, shit! His grandmother was home! He looked scared. He looked at both of us and said, "Y'all gotta jump!"

"We gotta jump? Nah, nigga' I ain't jumping nowhere!"

He said, "The last time my grandmother caught people in her house she called the police and they went to juvie. You better jump or we both gone be in trouble." I looked out the window and froze. He looked at me and said, "Desmond gone jump first, he's done this before then you jump after him, he will catch you." Desmond climbed out the window and jumped. He was a big dude and seemed to make it down without a scratch, but that was a long way down for me; I was too short. It was my turn to jump. I asked him if he was going to catch me, and he said yeah, so, I jumped! This nigga' stepped back and walked away! I landed in a rose bush. I thought my ankle was broken, but I got up and limped away quickly down the alley in the back of the house.

When I got to the end, I tried to put weight on my left ankle, and I couldn't. It hurt so bad. The pain stopped for a quick moment when I realized I left my purse with my bus fare and my books at Greg's house! How was I going to get home? I was going to get in so much trouble when Momma found out what happened. I had to come up with a plan and quick.

I limped fast and tried to take the alleys as much as I could so no one would see me skipping school. My mom knew everybody, and I looked like her, so they knew me. I made it to Lincolnway, and I saw Crystal's cousins and her uncle. They saw that I was hurt so they helped me. Her cousin

Tyrone always had a crush on me, so he offered to carry me on his back since I was limping, "You sure? I can try to make it, you don't have to do that," I said. He carried me four blocks until we got to his house and asked his dad if he could give me a ride home in his truck since my ankle was messed up. His dad did. Everyone asked how I broke my ankle. I told them I was running from a dog and managed to get away by jumping the fence and landed on my ankle, they believed me. Let's just hope Mom did too!

When I got home, I told my mom the story I'd made up. She immediately took me to the hospital. I stayed home from school for two days on the R.I.C.E. (rest, ice, circulation and elevation) diet. I was glad I didn't get in trouble for skipping school and that my story was believable, for now.

My mom called the school to let them know I would need special accommodations since I was on crutches. The principal didn't really like me, but she said that we could talk about it once my mom came to the school for a meeting. We met in Mrs. Williams's office and talked about the school's plan for my temporary handicap. After that was settled, Mrs. Williams said, "Ms. Green I have something for you. This appears to be Tarena's science book that was found by police officers on the other side of town. You might want to ask your daughter how it got there." My eyes got big and I knew I was busted!

Shit! I had to think quick and come up with something! It was getting hard to keep up with all these lies, but I told another one. "I let a friend borrow my books, she must have left them somewhere and someone found them." She believed it. Eventually she'd find out I was no longer a virgin, but not today. I think my mom may have lost her virginity at twelve too, I heard rumors from family members that before my mom had Twila she had miscarriages or abortions which meant she started sooner than fifteen. If this had blown up at some point, I was going to ask her how old she was when she lost her virginity. I'd hate to get in trouble for someone I wasn't that crazy about. I mean I liked Greg but, I really just wanted to lose my virginity to get it over with. I thought the longer I waited, the more it was going to hurt.

William Street- Summer 1997

I loved and hated the summer, the freedom of not going to school, light clothing, and hanging out with my friends late were things I looked forward to, but there was never enough to eat, and it was a guarantee that one or more of our utilities would be shut off. It wasn't a big deal when the electricity was off during the school year, because at least we had heat or air-conditioning at school. But when I didn't have anything to do all day and couldn't watch T.V., I had to make the best the of daylight hours. This summer the electricity and water were off. I learned quickly about survival over pride. Our water had been off most of the summer, so my mom started bringing home buckets of water so that we could flush the toilets and heat it up so that we could have hot water to wash up.

    I remember one day the entire house smelled like piss and shit. Mom had been gone for a couple days. When she got home, she wanted to know why we were sitting in this funky-ass house! I told her we had to go to the bathroom and that's why it stunk, because we couldn't flush the toilets.

    She said, "Y'all my kids, y'all need to learn how to survive. I know I taught y'all better than that. Come here to the window. When it stinks like that you gotta let some fresh air in, and you have to know where to go get the water. You see Mr. Jones's house right there? Well he has a faucet on the side of his house. Take these two buckets and your brother. Go over there and fill them up with water, bring them back so we can flush the toilets. But make sure you turn it tight when you are done. We can't have water leaking after we use it.

I told my mom I didn't want to do that because it was stealing! She said, "It ain't stealing if it's a kid doing it. I can't do it. But if he catches y'all doing it, he won't be mad at some kids." I said okay and got some water as quickly as possible. It seemed like it took forever for the buckets to fill up, and they were heavy, we struggled to get them back to our house. We flushed the toilets like that the rest of the summer until the water was turned back on by Portage Township, they helped underserved families . Thank goodness the water was back on right before school started. Now we could take showers and baths instead of having to wash up in the sink. Washing up in the sink, always felt dirty and degrading, maybe because I overheard my granny saying that it was a ho bath. Binky was so excited about the water he was taking two baths a day, just because he could.

William Street- Fall 1997 8th Grade

In eighth grade I really wanted to be on the cheer team. I wanted the respect, popularity, and the uniform that came with it, so I became friends with Mary Campbell. She was cool and was about the same height as me, 5'1," so I figured we would be good practice buddies. We practiced after school at her house in the backyard for several weeks until it was time for tryouts. Mrs. Williams, our principal, was one of the judges, along with the coaches and a freshman cheerleader from Clay High. I knew for a fact that no matter how good I did, I wasn't going to make it. Mrs. Williams almost got me caught up by giving my mom that book, and now she was a judge. At this point, I didn't have anything to lose, so I tried out anyway, and I didn't want to let Mary down.

We auditioned in pairs, and I must have hit the jackpot. The judges assigned the partners and mine just happened to be Mary! Thank goodness it was her! We had great chemistry and I felt like I would do great with someone I had already been practicing with. We both walked in, introduced ourselves, completed a cheer, a chant, and a jump of our choice and walked off with our fists on our hips. We nailed it! Now, it would be up to Mrs. Williams and the other judges to figure out who made the squad. They said results would be posted in the morning and to come back to the practice gym to see if our names made the list at the end of the first period.

The next day, when the first hour bell rang, I ran as fast as I could to see if my name was on the list, and it was!! Mary's name was on the list too! I couldn't wait to get home and tell my mom the news!

The bus rolled up to my stop, the front door of my house was open, and when I walked in there were clothes and papers all over the place. This was always a sign that my mom was looking for money she might have misplaced, and it meant that when she found it, she was going to get high. I ran through the house looking for her. She was in her room sitting on the floor going through her jean pockets. I pushed what she was doing out of my mind. "Mom guess what?"

She said, "You made the team, didn't you?" I proudly said yep! "I knew you would, you are my daughter, what else did they expect?" My mother spoke with such confidence about me and the pride she had in me, being her daughter. For the next few days, my mom told everybody that came to our house that her baby was on the cheerleading team, that I was smart, and an athlete just like she was.

William Street- Rat-Tail Comb – Late Fall 1997

All my life I endured the whispers and the comments about Twila's dad—Paul and her Aunt Paula. My aunties and cousins told me I looked just like Paul and Paula and that they knew he was my real daddy. Whenever anyone said anything about it, I said, "You must be out of your mind. My real daddy is David!" He been the only person I knew to be my daddy, even if he lived in another state, I knew he was my daddy. My Davis family loved me. They came and got me on the weekends and spent time with me and bought me things I needed. There was no way that me and Twila had the same dad. If we had the same dad, he wouldn't be coming to pick her up for the weekend and leave me behind; logically it didn't make sense to grab one of your kids and leave the other behind.

  One day, Twila asked me to go to church with her. She said her Granny and Grandpa Franklin wanted her to bring me. I didn't feel like being around a bunch of uppity church folk, but I went anyway because I always enjoyed spending time with my cool sister. I knew I'd get a good meal afterwards. Her grandmother, Mrs. Winston, seemed nice, but she asked a lot of questions, and one time asked me if I had some better stockings because mine had runs in them. I told her no, I don't have more stockings, and we ain't got no money to get anymore.

I figured she picked up on that and she let it go. After church she took us to get something to eat and then took us home. She said we could go to church with her every Sunday if we wanted to, I didn't really want to, who wants to go to church every Sunday?

Before I knew it, I was going to Sunday School and church every Sunday. After a while, I felt like I was doing something right with my life and that things were starting to fall into place. One day she said that Paul was going to pick us up for church and that we would spend some time with him, but I didn't like the way she said it. It sounded like a setup; after all, this was her son.

Me and Twila went to church with Paul. People kept commenting on how I looked just like him, and he kept smiling and saying thank you, instead of telling them that I wasn't his daughter. It made me uncomfortable and proud at the same time. It was weird. After church, he took us to get some food and then asked if we wanted to go get dessert. Twila seemed annoyed, so she said no. I said yeah, I wanted to go, he said he would drop Twila off and ask my mom if it was okay for me to go with him.

I overheard them talking. My mom said, "You know I ain't never had a problem with you trying to be a part of her life, yeah she can go with you." I was so happy. She was being nice, and it seemed like Paul was on my mom's good side. This became a thing. We hung out almost every weekend for a couple months. Something was bothering me though. I asked him if he was my real dad, but he never came right out and said it to me. I needed to know. I needed him to say the words. It seemed like we were making a lot of assumptions and I just needed to hear it. He said "Yes, I'm your real dad, you look just like me." I couldn't see it. I saw his pot belly, his big thighs, his facial hair, and bald head, and he even showed me scars from being born with extra pinkies. I was born with extra pinkies too. Maybe he was right, but what about my Davis family? Shouldn't they know the truth? Would they want to still be in my life if I told them? It'd been thirteen years. Why didn't my momma handle this when I was a baby? Would I have to pick which family I wanted?

I was scared to have this conversation. Why wasn't my mom doing it for me? Was she scared? Embarrassed? It'd been thirteen years. Surely, she'd had this conversation or at least thought about it. I'd do her the favor and just write my granny a letter. She deserved to know. After all, I didn't need her anymore. I still loved her, but now that my real dad was in my life, he could take care of me like he took care of Twila.

In that letter I told my granny that I loved her, but I needed to build a relationship with my real dad, and that we both had extra pinkies, and that everyone said that I looked just like him, so I must be his, right? A few months went by, and I didn't get a response. She didn't write me back. Maybe she didn't get it or maybe she was mad at me.

A week later, I was home alone with my mom. Binky was out playing with his friends, and Twila was at work at the beauty salon downtown. She was the shampoo girl and was learning all about the shop. It was about two o'clock in the afternoon and I was upstairs listening to music in Twila's room. I wasn't supposed to be touching her stuff or she would beat me up, but this day I didn't care. I was bored. I heard someone knocking on the door, so I went downstairs and it was this guy. He looked like he was the same age as Twila, his hair was all over his head, and he said he was there to see my mom. I got her and they went upstairs.

A few minutes later my mom yelled, "Tarena, bring down that rat tail comb, I need it so that I can do his hair." I don't know what took over me. But somebody had to say something to her, there always seemed to be a trickledown effect when she was getting high. I was tired of being without the things we needed, and being made fun of at school because of it, and for damn sure was tired of having people in our house that didn't belong there! I had it! She was not getting high today, not if I have anything to do with it!

I yelled, "No, I'm not giving you this comb, all you going to do is get high."

She came upstairs and said, "Come here, what you just say?"

I stuck my chest out. "I *said*, I'm not giving you my comb, because when you finish doing his hair, you going to do drugs." Before I knew it, I couldn't see. My mom was attacking me like I was a stranger on the street. I was taking punches to my head, face, stomach, and ribs. All I could do was ball up and hope that she would stop. There was blood everywhere. I thought my nose was broken, and my sides hurt so bad. She told me to get up and clean up my mess and go to my room and shut the fuck up. She told me if she heard me crying, she would come upstairs and throw me out the window. She was serious. The way she just beat my ass, I knew she wasn't playing. I went to my room, grabbed a pillow, and put my face in it and cried hard. I called my dad, I mean Paul. I called him at his work number, and he told me to take a deep breath and I told him what happened. He said that I should call the police, she had no reason to jump on me up like that. I called the police; it took them forever to get to our house. By the time they got there my mom was done with that dude's hair, and they were gone. My white t-shirt didn't have a white spot on it, it was soaked in blood. Twila had gotten off work and was horrified that the police were there.

They asked us if we had somewhere to go, because if they found my mom she was going to jail for what she did to me. The police knew my mom by name—Janette Green. We called Mrs. Winston, Twila's granny, well, *our* granny. She said we could stay with her for a little while, so the police drove us to her house. Binky was going to stay with his friends. When we got there, she told us the rules, and that we had to go to church several times a week, shower, and not to get her house dirty. I liked structure but this was a bit much, but it felt good to have someone care, and be willing to take us in. Paul couldn't take us because he was staying with his father, I guess my grandfather. A couple days went by, and Child Protective Services called Mrs. Winston. They were coming to do an interview. I asked them if my mom had to be there and they said she needed to know that I was being interviewed but she wouldn't be in the room.

The next day, they showed up and my mom was there too. I didn't feel comfortable. Why was she there? When the case worker opened her notebook, I thought we were going to move to another room so that we could talk alone. My mom said, "Anything you need to say to my daughter you can say in front of me." The case worker looked scared. I don't blame her. My mom could be that way sometimes. My mom gave me the look, the one that said, you better not say anything that's going to get me in trouble. I could hear her in my head: *What happens in our house stays in our house!*

I told the case worker that my mom didn't hit me and that I called the police because I was mad. She asked me if I was sure, and I said yes, and looked to my mom for approval. She said, "Well that's all, I don't see any reason why you can't take your girls home with you today." What? Just like that? We were going home? What if I didn't want to go? They didn't really want to help us, the case worker nor my grandmother really cared, they were both there out of obligation, not because they cared. As we packed, I recall Mrs. Winston saying that she done raised her kids and she was too old to be raising somebody else's. I'll never forget those words. We left with our belongings and walked to the bus stop to go home with our mom. As we walked, she reminded me that this was all my fault that she went to jail and that these white people from Child Protective Services were all in our business, and that she had to come all the way across town for this shit. But it was not my fault she beat me up me over a comb! Over a comb so she could get high.

William Street- Gone and Be with them People- Winter 1997

It was almost winter, and our electricity had been out for a couple weeks, and we were using space heaters to stay warm. We had water but no way to heat it, so we had to use an electric skillet and put a pot of water on it to heat it up so we can wash up in the mornings before school. I wanted to go school, it was the one place I was warm and could eat at least twice a day. We had a new social worker at school. His name was Mark Smith. He kind of reminded me of Santa Claus but younger. He was nice, and one of my teachers suggested that I visit him once a week if I needed someone to talk to.

I wanted to tell him something. I didn't want to get anyone in trouble, but I knew that we couldn't go on the way that we had been. Someone needed to know what was going on. Our mom had been in jail for three weeks. She called us collect and told us she didn't have anyone that could get her out, so she was going to sit out her bail. She didn't tell us what she was in there for, but she did say it wasn't her fault. I went to see Mark after the lunch period.

I told him that we didn't have any food at home, no heat, and my mom hadn't been home for three weeks. She was going to be home soon, but I didn't want to be there when she came home. We were old enough to be at home alone, I was thirteen, Twila was sixteen, and Binky was ten. I knew that when she got out, she was going to be mean to us, because of the withdrawals she had from drugs. Mark asked me if there was someone I could stay with. I told him I wanted to go stay with my Granny Jewell. She probably wouldn't take me since I wrote her that letter a few months ago saying she wasn't my granny. Paul was supposed to be our dad, but he didn't help us, and neither did Mrs. Winston because she had raised all her kids. My last hope was my Granny Jewell.

Mark said, "Tarena, *if* you refuse to go home, I can't make you go. But *you have* to refuse to go. Do you refuse to go home?"

I said "Yes! I refuse to go home."

He said, "What's your grandmother's phone number?" They talked for a little bit and then he said she wanted to talk to me.

She said, "Tarena, I got your letter, and you are just a child, there is so much you don't know. We have people in our family with extra pinkies and you look very much like us too, and you always been ours and will always be ours no matter what. I wanted to tell you that before you got over here. Tell Mr. Smith you can come and stay with me for as long as you want to. You are *my* granddaughter and as long as I have a roof over my head so do you!" I said thank you and gave him the phone so that he could get directions to her apartment.

When he hung up, I cried. "I can't believe she still loves me and still wants me to come live with her after the mean things I said to her." Mark wiped my tears and told me to get my things from my locker. He was taking me to my granny's house. On the way to my granny's he stopped at the store, grabbed some laundry detergent and a few groceries and told me that he wanted to help. He pulled up to my granny's apartment. I got out and slowly walked up the stairs to her apartment, with tears in my eyes. When she opened the door, she gave me the biggest hug. I knew I was home. I was getting settled in later that evening when Twila called and told me that Mom was just released from jail and was home. She and Binky never left the house, so I imagined she'd make me come back. I was hoping I could enjoy this moment, this night, without having to face my mom or go back with her.

The next day, Granny called my mom because they ain't never had no problem with each other, and she wanted her to know that she had me and would take care of me until she got on her feet. I was sitting on the other side of the room, and could hear my mom yelling, "She ain't never gotta go up to that school, telling those white folks my business, what happens in my house stays in my house, since she wants to run her mouth and tell my business, she ain't welcome over here no more. Jewell you can stop by my house tomorrow. I'll have a letter waiting for you, signing over full custody of Tarena; she is your problem now!" And she hung up. My granny knew that I had heard the full conversation. Just like that she could sign over her rights? I cried myself to sleep that night. But I was safe from harm, my belly full, and I was warm. I hoped my granny wouldn't get rid of me too.

CPSIA information can be obtained
at www.ICGtesting.com
Printed in the USA
LVHW110201040422
715236LV00005B/404

9 798674 229049